PLOTTING
GREAT
OUTCOMES

PLOTTING GREAT OUTCOMES

HEWAD POPAL
IMRAN POPAL

DEDICATION

We are grateful for our Mom, who is the GPS of the family; our Baba, who is the system's troubleshooter, and our dear brother Sohaib, a much-needed circumnavigator for everyone; and, finally and equally, Mr. William R. Gower, for his unconditional love and support.

INTRODUCTION

Plotting Great Outcomes advocates thoughtfulness before action, productivity over occupation, and results over reports.

No idea in this book is indispensable—but all are indisputable.

CONTENTS

CHARACTER/MINDSET

BE THE BEST VERSION OF YOURSELF

No specific mold will shape you into a flawless person. Different people define "great" and "success" in a thousand different ways. To be a great "you," you must start with the basics. You must commit to practicing healthy habits.

It is an adage that a healthy mind starts with a healthy body. Taking good care of yourself is the foundation for being a useful and productive member of your family and society. Having a firm guide and discipline is equally important. For some, this could mean spiritual guidance or meditation. For others, this could mean going to a park, enjoying nature and getting a breath of fresh air. There is no one preferred path. It depends entirely on what feels right for every individual.

Next time you look in the mirror, close your eyes and ask yourself when you feel like the best version of you. When you open them, act on that.

— Leandra Medine

HABITS

Habits start when your thinking leads to an action. Once you start practicing the act, good or bad, you then adopt a particular pattern.

There are many examples of bad habits: sleeping late, eating unhealthy food, and so on. One of the most significant adverse habits I had was procrastination. Procrastination is not something that you can deal with right away. I had a lot of trouble with it, and occasionally, I still do. These distractions can come in the form of your electronic devices, friends and even family, sometimes. To get rid of the bad habit first, I put myself in an environment where I was able to put away all my distractions easily. Secondly, I made sure that I had a solid goal to fulfill, and that's when I started to lose my bad habit. It was harder than it seemed, but once I got a good rhythm for the work I was doing, I dropped my bad habit.

An example of a better habit comes from Imran. From a very young age, Imran had a good habit of being committed to what he did—and that was soccer. Soccer kept him physically fit and mentally upbeat. He was practicing soccer with little support or encouragement from anyone, and soccer was and fortunately remains his real passion. But somewhere along the line, Imran was distracted by another sport, which was American football.

Football is the most popular sport in the U.S. At the time, the Seattle Seahawks started winning one game after another, and it was becoming clear that they were headed to the Super Bowl. Since we live in Seattle, we were among Seahawk supporters. Imran drifted away from soccer and more toward football and became, along with a lot of Seattleites, "The 12th Man." While the Seahawks were making progress, our brother was lagging in soccer. He was playing football video games and watching football on television. Imran's good habits changed to bad ones. Fortunately, while the Seahawks' winning the Super Bowl marked the end of the American football season, it was the kickoff of Imran's regaining interest in practicing soccer.

The lesson and advice we want to share with you is to remain committed to practicing your good habits even when you are in a tempting environment. Don't become complacent, because complacency is the enemy of a "good you."

Just like bad habits, good habits will shape your future. Carry on enjoying yourself and your time with friends and acquaintances, but never let procrastination cost you your long-term goals and dreams.

**We are what we repeatedly do. Excellence,
then, is not an act, but a habit.**

— Aristotle

BAD PRACTICES BECOME BAD ADDICTIONS

Since the early 2000s, there has been constant innovation in the software and hardware industry to generate learning and entertainment tools for kids and young adults. We must acknowledge that some of these hardware tools, software apps, and programs have significantly helped people learn about the world around them and helped find the answers to some difficult questions. Equally, these innovations have been a vital source of entertaining times and entertainment with our peers as well as with our parents and relatives.

On the other hand, these modes of entertainment have become dangerously addictive, and they have become a primary source of ill health and a massive hurdle to progress. While my brothers and I are not savvy with computer programs nor experts with the hardware entertainment tools, we can testify—with complete confidence based on first-hand experience—that daily slots of entertainment can become hours of addiction. For example, the day before we started writing this section, our parents had guests from France for the whole day. They had to go out all day while we sat at home, surrounded by many electronics. We had a choice of using this situation to our advantage, entertaining ourselves and not learning anything, or we could have used it for learning and discovering new things while still using it for fun. And guess what we did? Yup, without a second guess, we used the electronics to entertain us, without even giving any time for something productive or even finishing tasks we had to do.

We used the electronics for about three hours straight before having to get up unwillingly, since we had to go to the bathroom. After our bathroom break was over, we were tired of the very entertainment we had once so willingly desired. Between us, there was a realization that we'd wasted our time.

Our mom came home and saw the house was exactly the way it had been. Our homework remained undone. Before any of us could greet her or say a word, she had counted down from five, and right away all three of us cleaned everything.

An hour could be a good investment in anything, so choose how to use your time wisely. That's not to say that entertaining yourself doesn't have its merits, but moderation is a prerequisite for discipline. And self-education will steer you away from practices that may lead to harmful addictions.

Greatness is not a function of circumstance. Greatness, it turns out, is largely a matter of conscious choice, and discipline.

—James C. Collins,
Good to Great: *Why Some Companies Make the Leap ...and Others Don't*

SELF-DISCIPLINE

The best example we know of self-discipline is our mother. We aren't just saying this because she is someone we love, but for us, she is the definition of self-discipline.

Knowing when to do what and not being distracted or influenced are her two main specialties. Many people, like family and friends, tell her things like, "You work too hard," "You need to relax more," "Your kids will be fine," or "They will learn themselves." And they also advise many other things—which isn't ever a one-time thing. Most of the time, our mom drove us back from soccer practice or a game or from school and many other outings; the list could be quite long. People saw this and commented that she worked too hard. Now, as a mother, you are thinking one of two things, 1) "I work hard, and they are right: I should take a break" or 2) "No, as a mother, this is my job and later, my kids will thank me and realize how much I have done for them." Our mom always chose the second approach. She knew that working hard and having a full commitment now would help her children grow with love and confidence. Our mother already feels the appreciation we have for her efforts.

It is essential to know when to do what and to know right from wrong. Those two things will lead to a life of success. If you have something to do, set up a time, and finish it. Fulfilling tasks based on priorities will relieve you from stressing and trying to do several things at once. If you determine right from wrong now, it will serve you well in the future. Frankly, many of us—even when knowing the right thing and knowing the consequence of the wrong—still do the wrong thing. I will be the first to admit this because we all are guilty of it to some extent. Thus, it is best to accept our shortcomings, learn from them and fix them. Perfection is not the aim here. We will make mistakes occasionally, but some level of discipline will help us to maintain the right path.

There is no specific way to learn self-discipline other than practicing and encouraging yourself to step up and choose the right option in any given circumstance. The example we presented to you is about our mom, but the moral of what she does is that you will have distractions: friends and peers will pressure you into having fun and doing things instead of working towards whatever your goal might be. Work smart and hard now to have fun in the long run.

With self-discipline most anything is possible.

—Theodore Roosevelt

COMPETE
WITH YOURSELF

Often it is not others who fail us; nor is it the circumstances of our own lives. Instead, within each of us, the inner-self is the enemy that prevents us from accomplishing great things. We must make our opportunities and chances because there will never be a "just right moment." Telling yourself to wait for that moment is akin to wasting your time. It's not staying true to yourself, but instead harming yourself. You can make excuses that will negatively affect your future, or you can be a person who takes responsibility into your own hands. The choice is yours, just as it is for the rest of us. How we go about doing that involves competing with ourselves, forbidding the temptation of an easy way to cause us to drift off our path.

We can trick someone else, but once faced with the reality of what is in front of us, we can never trick or fool ourselves. I was the most unrealistic person I knew, not to others but to myself. And it was the worst thing I could do to myself, given how much I would sweep under the rug. That stuff wasn't just going away by itself; it would pile up to where I couldn't ignore it. You know what that stuff was? Loss. Loss of competition against myself. Yes;

sometimes, I tried my best, and at some point, you may have done so as well. You competed with yourself, and you did everything you could have done, but you still didn't get what you wanted. If you give up before you start, you never would have even had a chance, and when the time passes by, you will always wonder--what if I had tried? Success results from your previous efforts just as the lack of it is due to inaction. So, keep up with the competition and win every battle against yourself in the game we call life.

Look in the mirror. That is your competition.

—Unknown [CA10]

BEING TRUE
TO YOURSELF

Too many of us know what the truth is but never act upon it. I watched a movie called "The Scent of a Woman." It was a great movie, but what stuck with me was when Frank Slade (Al Pacino) spoke out to the committee before him. Near the end of the speech he said:

"Now I have come to the crossroads in my life. I always knew what the right path was without exception. I knew. But I never took it. You know why? It was too damn hard."

When I first listened to the speech, I was amazed at how great of a statement it was. I liked the movie so much because I could feel a sense of relation to what those sentences meant. I knew how it felt because I, too, have been in similar circumstances. When I was true to myself, I could feel the difference between temporary happiness and satisfaction. However, whenever I chose the wrong path, I would get small benefits right away, but eventually, I would never feel satisfied. When I chose the right path, I neither felt happy nor satisfied right away, but ultimately, I would feel both satisfaction and happiness.

When you are true to yourself, you look at things realistically.

Meanwhile, being unrealistic with yourself will make you live a pretended life. It is a fairytale of running away from the truth that will catch up to you anyways. With this approach, you drag yourself down. And when you do that, in the end, there will be no one to blame but yourself.

I have a close friend I know like a brother. I've been friends with him for about five years. This man has a lot of potential in life and is smart. Even a stranger would notice his good qualities. I know his strengths and his weaknesses. The possibility this man has is perpetually being destroyed because of the lack of clarity he has about himself. He hides from the truth and tries to cover it up, and because of this, he is having trouble in his life. Many people have tremendous potential, but until they realize their possibilities, they won't make any substantial progress.

By being true to yourself, you can build a character that will be happier in the long run and ready to face both opportunities and obstacles with confidence.

A lot of the conflicts in your life exist because you're not living in alignment; you're not true to yourself.

—Steve Maraboli,
Unapologetically You: Reflections of Life and the Human Experience

DON'T FORGET
YOUR PAST

I've failed a lot in my seventeen years. I've failed not at everything, but a lot of things. It sucks to fail, and it's even worse to fail at the same thing a second or third time.

You will face many tough challenges throughout your life, as everyone does. But that doesn't give you the right to give up.

We should take inspiration from children. They are so damn amazing. There are three unique qualities children have, and as we grow, most of us will lose them. First, children are great at being persistent. If a child wants to annoy the crap out of someone, man, they will do everything in their power to do so, and they will likely succeed. As toddlers grow, they attempt to walk. They fall for days and weeks trying to walk, but eventually, they walk. Their persistence is admirable. They will remain focused until they complete what they want to achieve.

Second, think of children's obliviousness to everything; they don't waste their time overthinking. When little boys or girls want something, they don't dwell on how hard it will be to get. They will do what they must do to get it. While we are growing older, we tend to lose the tenacity we had as children. Instead, we focus on how hard it is to get something.

Third, children take chances. Some of those chances end up being risky. However, with a majority of the chances kids take, they end up being satisfied. It is essential that we all maintain some level of all three of these qualities. They were inherently part of us as children. Those of us who maintain them are considered some of the most highly accomplished individuals.

> It's okay to celebrate success, but it is more important to heed the lessons of failure.
>
> **—Bill Gates**

NEVER BE AFRAID OF SETBACKS

FAILURE IS INEVITABLE

As a young adult, your life will evolve around the ages of 14 to 20, which will likely be the most fluid and uncertain time of your life. You are figuring out yourself and your aspirations and adjusting to new schools, work environments and friends.

A lot of young adults fear disappointment and failing at fulfilling tasks and deadlines. That makes it harder for them to start doing something meaningful.

Whoever you are, you must remember to be ready for potential setbacks. Embrace them and learn from them. Failures point out your shortcomings and highlight areas in need of improvement. Don't be afraid to try something new unless you know it can be harmful. If it's something like a new sport, go for it.

Be prepared for failure as you might not get it the first time, and you won't be the best at it the moment you get into it. It takes a courageous effort and a big push to try something new. Of course, you may not like everything you try. That's fine. Try something else. If you do something new and fail at it the first time, don't just quit. Learn from that mistake and change it into motivation to do better next time. There was a time when I disliked soccer. I am a competitive person by nature. I feared being the worst, and I wasn't used to the fact that everybody was better than me. Reluctantly, I kept playing with a little push from my younger brother, Imran. So, for the first six months, I didn't see praiseworthy improvements. Then, on month seven I saw progress in my playing ability. I felt better about the game, and I slowly grew to have a passion for it. It took time for me to notice I wasn't the only one stagnant. Most players were in the same position as I was, but we were also slowly progressing. Realizing this made me feel more comfortable playing.

A lot of us are procrastinators, excuse makers, and people who settle for what comes our way. That's the truth. We think that our success will come from one push of effort, and it will magically fall into our laps. It is, in fact, the complete opposite. There will be setbacks, there will be obstacles, and sometimes, you will want to let go of what you desire. If you take a deep breath and assess the situation, tell yourself that you can try a different way, maybe the next time, you will get the thing you want. We will never know until we try one extra time. That one extra push may be the last thing you need to get what you want. So never fear setbacks, use them as a lesson, and keep pushing.

It is impossible to live without failing at something unless you live so cautiously that you might as well not have lived at all, in which case you have failed by default.

—J. K. Rowling

DON'T LET
ANYTHING STOP YOU

You decide whether you get distracted by something; you decide if you slack on things; you decide if you will use excuses your whole life and let every little thing interfere with what you must accomplish. You also choose to strive, persevere and achieve. The most hardened person to deal with is yourself.

You will be the one itching to have fun when instead you must get work done. When achieving the bigger goals and dreams, sometimes, the odds will be entirely against you. Sometimes, you will look at the situation you're in, and it will look like there is no way you will get to your goal.

The thought in your head will drag you towards negativity and you might even conclude that achieving what you want is impossible. In reality, this is the exact time when you should get up and do what you must.

It's difficult. If it weren't, everybody would be doing it. Once you turn it into a habit and work from one small achievement to another, you will see results.

No matter how big or small the goal, do everything in your power to achieve it and let nothing get in your way.

Success is not final; failure is fatal: it is the courage to continue that counts.

—Winston Churchill

YOUR ATTITUDE WILL SET
THE OUTCOME OF YOUR DAY

Attitude is a fundamental part of life. It is the force behind any outcome and it sets the tone for your encounters. Your attitude can even shape who you are as a person, and it can shape your life, whether it's for better or worse.

It all starts with your mornings. Some people don't realize the importance of the first few moments after they wake up and how it can shape the flow of their entire day. When you wake up in the morning and your attitude is positive, chances are, you will remain positive throughout the entire day, and people around you will notice it. If you start with a poor mood in the morning, you will likely display negativity throughout the whole day. Whether your attitude is lousy or positive, it is often your choice, and you will wear it as a badge.

Notice how a friend's attitude will rub off on you. If your friends are confident and have a positive mindset, it will quickly—without your realizing—rub off on you. If they don't have a positive mindset, chances are, your attitude will turn negative.

We are not flawless. There were many times when I had a lousy and negative attitude. I would often think I was a victim of every situation and thought I deserved better.

Whether I deserved better or not didn't matter. What mattered was that my attitude of feeling as if I was a victim was wrong. I often notice a similar feeling of disappointment among some of my peers. I've seen young adults my age always make themselves feel like a victim in so many situations when they aren't. Since I was around these types of people, I started putting myself down for no apparent reason.

Our attitude is in our control, and we must shape and keep it healthy. Otherwise, not only will our day be filled with negativity, but our lives may also end up negative.

Whether you think you can or you think
you can't, you're right.

— Henry Ford

ADMITTING REALITY

An Afghan saying states, "The truth is sour and spicy." Sometimes, it's tough to face the truth; but eventually, we must. It's the end destiny. We don't like admitting our faults or facing our reality because, frankly, it's too unpleasant. Many of us allow this feeling of shame or false pride from knowing we're wrong to get the best of us. We run away from the reality and problems in our lives and let denial overtake us. It is hard when we are—rightfully—criticized and are told of our shortcomings. It makes us upset, and it makes us argumentative.

If you know you are at fault, if you know you have done something wrong, and if you know that the truth is just the truth, then face it, because eventually, you will. Instead of not admitting something and arguing more, accept it. You will be the bigger person in the end. Submitting to the truth is far better than disputing it. You can learn from it, and then move on. The time you would waste on arguing with another person can be used for improving yourself.

A man must be big enough to admit his mistakes, smart enough to profit from them, and strong enough to correct them.

— John C. Maxwell

DON'T CONFUSE PRODUCTIVITY WITH BOREDOM

Do you ever wonder why you get so bored doing the things that are the most beneficial for your future? Why is it that we wait until the last minute to do things that we know we should carry out now? It is best to give up your immediate pleasure for results that come in later and last longer. On the flip side, going out and having fun with family and friends is something that everyone can enjoy. Therefore, we often confuse productivity with boredom.

Productivity can be misconceived. It's repetitive, but it leads to a lasting outcome. For example, working toward a degree or working hard for your family is repetitive, but it is beneficial for your future. Often, people end up taking what they have for granted, and the very opportunities they have been handed go to waste because of a person's lack of appreciation for them.

**Productivity is never an accident.
It is always the result of a commitment to excellence,
intelligent planning, and focused effort.**

— Paul Meyer

TAKE PRIDE IN
THE RIGHT THINGS

People are prideful about their culture, their country, the area in which they live and their accomplishments. We are rightfully prideful about our family and friends.

Pride can be a great asset, but it can also be a self-initiating problem. At times, I have seen people have a false sense of pride. They are proud of things of which they shouldn't be. For example, some young adults pride themselves in getting angry about other people's opinions that are not similar to theirs. Other young adults pride themselves on not responding to their peers' requests for help. There are others that pride themselves on creating and winning arguments. None of these behaviors is something we should be proud of; in fact, it's a waste of time just contemplating it.

Let's take pride in the things that matter.

It was pride that changed the angels into devils;
It is humility that makes men as angels

— Saint Augustine.

DON'T LET YOUR FEELINGS TAKE OVER YOUR LOGIC

Emotions and feelings are a part of us. You are going to feel different emotions: happy, sad, angry, grateful, ungrateful, and so on. Remembering to not base our decisions on these momentary emotions is the key that will prevent us from trouble.

When you're emotional, in a way, you aren't yourself. Our thoughtfulness and reasoning are preferable to our emotional reactions. However, when our emotions fuel our actions, we come across as random and unexpected. When our emotions are at their highest, our reasoning becomes unreliable because of these moments.

In times of sadness and anger, you will likely say and do things you genuinely don't mean. I have said unpleasant things to my older brother, which I neither meant nor wanted to say. Those reactions were all due to the emotions I felt at the moment.

Uncontrolled emotions can cause you big troubles. The story I am about to share with you is about a young man whose emotion cost him his life. He was driving on a freeway when another driver cut in front of him. He became emotional and took revenge by cutting in front of the same driver. The two got into a tense argument and decided to pull over. As soon as they got to a stop, the other driver pulled out a gun and shot the young man in the head. This altercation and the unfortunate situation could have easily been avoided if the boy had just ignored the other driver's offense. Instead of making a fatal decision while angry, he could have just ignored it.

You may agree that whenever we are angry with someone or feel sad, we say things or do things we never mean, but some fail to recognize this also happens when people are excited or overjoyed.

Similar circumstances will be handed to everyone at some point in life, and whether the choice made is logical or emotional depends on the individual. We must remember that every decision may come with a reward or a consequence. Never make a decision based on momentary emotions.

No matter the situation, never let your emotions overpower your intelligence.

—Unknown

ADDING VS. ELIMINATING

It's easy to add more to your life such as new friends, acquaintances or activities. It is hard to do the opposite: getting rid of friends or acquaintances and not having too much fun.

It is satisfying to have more of just about anything because that creates excitement. We rarely cut anything out of our lives because having more things is sometimes inaccurately correlated to more fulfillment. Eliminating fun is much harder than participating in it, wouldn't you agree? Most of the time, the excess activities that we add to our lives are destructive and detrimental to our primary goals. They suck up most of our time and efforts.

There was a time where I couldn't distinguish the right kind of friend from the wrong kind. I decided to meet new people and to add them to my life. Soon, I got acquainted with the wrong people, and eventually, I became friends with them. They were not bad people, but they were people that would drag my positivity down. At one point, my uncle gave me advice that sticks with me to this day:

"When I was in high school, I was at the peak of my life. Not only was I in the best shape physically, but mentally I was untouchable as well. I didn't have many friends, but once I started to excel in my life, my peers wanted to surround me. Being naive and ignorant, I decided to befriend all of them. It backfired on me so much because all their negativity and lack of their self-fulfillment dragged me down. They saw the positivity I had, and they wanted it as well because they couldn't obtain it themselves. Like leeches, they sucked at my success eventually draining me, my time, and my future."

After I heard this, I not only eliminated most of my so-called friends, but I stopped hanging around them and focused on myself, my own life and my future. You must thoughtfully evaluate who your good friends are and then have the courage to eliminate the rest.

In many ways life is about managing your delusions; keeping the ones that nourish and eliminating the ones that poison

— Steve Maraboli

MAKING
WISE CHOICES

I took a class in eighth grade about decision-making. It was a one-day class explaining how you can always make a smart and unemotional decision. Whether you face a tough obstacle or two tempting routes, and you don't know which one to choose, there is always a proper decision to be made in any circumstance. The course was mainly focused on the significance and the long-term effect of making any decision, good or bad. The course had a lot of keywords, and the one word that still affects me today is "alternative."

When making a decision—depending on circumstances—there are a lot of emotional and outside distractions. For instance, there could be pressure from family, friends or a husband or wife. Then there's the situational pressure, meaning the amount of time you have to consider. There could also be the possibility of your fate or choosing to sacrifice one thing for the other.

Such circumstance makes it immensely difficult to pursue one very narrow decision. This class taught us to focus not only on what is there but also on what isn't. It was argued that there are always more than one or two options when facing a very tough time or decision in your life.

It's important to consider other alternatives when making any decision. It's essential to train your mind to think calmly under any circumstance.

Creative thinking inspires ideas. Ideas inspire change.

—Barbara Januszkiewicz

DO THE WORK NOW

Previously, we talked about the importance of choices and alternatives. Now, implementing our choices are done one of two ways. Take it easy at the start and rush fulfilling your commitments later. Or, take the first step right away and keep going. As the saying goes: "Slow is smooth, smooth is fast." When we finally pick our choice, we often are faced with two options of fulfilling it. One is to get on with the work and keep going until the job is complete. The other one is taking it easy at the beginning and dealing with everything at the end.

I cannot dictate or judge which option would be best for you, but in my experience, tackling the difficult parts early on is better. Later, you will have time to evaluate your work and make necessary adjustments.

A friend admitted to me, with a regretful face, "I wish I could go back to my freshman year of high school." He told me that a person he knew decided to not associate with others for the first two years of his high school life. My friend, at that time, thought that high school comes once, and he lived by that saying. The student that he was talking about ignored this motto and gave up his first two years of high school, waiting until his junior year. He dedicated all his time to his priorities in those two years, knowing that the time would pass by quickly. When his junior year rolled around, he was academically ahead of all of his peers, and he played soccer and tennis and excelled at both. Everyone else who was living by the saying "high school only comes once" was now looking up at him as a role model.

Whichever decision you make, either way, you'll end up facing the toughest parts. If you have fun at the start the tasks you must deal with will remain.

Sometimes the right path is not the easiest one.

—Pocahontas

MOST BAD THINGS
ARE PREVENTABLE

Undesirable circumstances occur just as good ones do. Life is not stationary. While we strive to deal with unfavorable situations, we forget to realize that some problems are self-created. From time to time, a problem is created as a result of our action or inaction. Self-created issues are preventable provided that we have done our homework and preparation prior to taking action. Thinking before making a controversial or uncertain action is and must remain the foundation.

We cannot solve our problems with the same thinking we used to create them

- Albert Einstein

GREAT
VS. RELEVANT

Our societies are obsessed with "great things" and "great people." Naturally, we are inclined to look for and get "great things" and want to become "great." Well, greatness often means rare or extraordinarily expensive when it comes to physical items. Great personalities have extraordinarily rare or unique accomplishments. So, to acquire extraordinarily expensive things, one must have or earn lots of wealth. And to achieve extraordinary accomplishments, one would need to have a clear vision, solid commitment and perseverance. Often, great things result from tough and precise work resulting in uncompromised quality. Similarly, great people have invested huge chunks of their lives into what makes them "great." The simple but true answer to understanding both is not the great things or great acts themselves. Rather, look at what went into making a thing "great" and becoming "great." So, you must not merely look to acquire great things but instead acquire relevant skills to earn you lots of wealth to be able to acquire significant items. Equally, you must not think about becoming a great person. Instead, pursue a path relevant and true to your vision that will make you become a great person.

What seems great may not be important; what seems relevant may be great eventually. Therefore, don't pursue greatness, hunt what is relevant.

Never let the urgent crowd out the important.

—Kelly Catlin Walker

DEFINE YOUR SUCCESS

Many people mistake the meaning of success. Commonly, people define success by being extremely rich, having a big house, car, and swimming pool, and so on, correct? We've heard people use the word, saying they want to be successful, and instantly, most of us think about having a few expensive items that right now, we only wish to have.

You want to pursue, achieve, and live the word, but that seems to be nearly impossible.

Now, the actual meaning of the word success is "the accomplishment of an aim or purpose." It means that success can range from learning to ride a bike or learning something new. You create a goal, beyond material wealth, and then achieve it.

Define success on your terms, achieve it by your own rules, and build a life you're proud to live.

—Anne Sweeney

YOUR RELATIONSHIPS
AND SURROUNDINGS

GENUINE RELATIONSHIPS

Genuine relationships are like a beehive in which everyone is in harmony with one another and strives for common good. Building strong bonds and total trust with your family members will cement a path of love and faith for the rest of your life. You must earn mutual and cherished dependability, especially when making important decisions. The foundation must have one component: Genuineness.

Life is not just a series of calculations and a sum of statistics; it's about experiences, it's about participation, it is something more complex and more interesting than what is obvious.

—Daniel Libeskind

PUT YOURSELF IN OTHER PEOPLE'S SHOES

Our world is full of amazing and bright people. These are people who strive to better themselves every day and to make our world a better place. Occasionally, we encounter stubborn and ignorant people. Everyone sees the world from his or her own viewpoint.

As such, people decide for themselves what is right or wrong, and they judge based on their exposures, experiences and standards. Therefore, we are all accustomed to judging things and others based on our standards, disregarding the complexities surrounding others.

Often, in conversations or debates, we are self-centered and stick to our opinions, even though they can sometimes be misguided. There is one simple and commonly known solution: Be open-minded and put yourself in other people's shoes. There are times I remember thinking that I was 100% right when I wasn't.

Train yourself to consider other people's opinion and concerns. Simply become a good listener. If the person is right, you will have given yourself the opportunity to learn something you didn't know before. Alternatively, you will become more confident in your position. You are rewarded either way.

Always put yourself in others' shoes.
If you feel it hurts you, it probably hurts the other person,
too.

—Rachel Grady

YOUR SENSES, ENVIRONMENT AND CONTACTS

What you hear, see, and say, the clothes you wear, and the food you eat will all shape who you will become. Let's see how they play a role in shaping yourself.

Hearing: If you socialize with intelligent people, you will become intelligent. If you socialize with people that are slackers, you, too, will become a slacker. Watch who you socialize with; their personalities will most likely rub off on you and vice versa.

We'll give you the example of our dad. Our dad's friends were sometimes twice as senior as he is and highly accomplished in their careers, so they were simultaneously his friends and mentors. By socializing with them, he learned a lot about business and life in general. Our dad would share with us the stories and experiences of these friends.

He would often give us books, articles and CDs on a variety of subjects that his friends had shared with him. It doesn't mean he became just like them, but he learned and adopted many of the excellent and useful things they knew and had gained over their lifetimes. Because our dad passed these lessons on, we learned and adapted these valuable lessons at a much earlier age than would have been possible otherwise. So, we knew more than our peers did about diverse subjects and disciplines in life. It shows that even your parent's friends can affect you.

Seeing: When we were about eight and six years old, we watched the Hulk movie. Hulk was and still is our favorite Marvel character, so we were hyped up after watching the movie. As soon as the movie ended, we started imitating the Hulk by throwing pillows and smashing them into things. We got so into it that we threw a pillow with no control at all, and it hit the window (I'm not saying who it was, because I'm not a snitch!). Luckily, it didn't shatter the window, but the outcome could have been dangerous on a cold London day. The movie itself wasn't terrible, but it affected how we behaved right after.

It goes for us now as well. Whenever we see something on our phones and tablets, and even things that our friends or family do, sometimes, we also crave to do the same thing. There are many cases when I have been outside and seen people eating, and I get hungry just by watching them, even if I already had something to eat 30 minutes earlier. If you watch a motivational video, you will feel motivated. If you watch someone who has a depressing attitude, that attitude will rub off on you as well. It all depends; be smart about what you keep your eyes on.

Saying: What you're saying is usually a response to what you're hearing, watching or experiencing. You are making a statement and/or expressing your feelings. When you make a statement repeatedly, or act in response to your circumstance in a certain manner, or use particular vocabularies, it will soon become a habit and later mold into your personality. It can happen either in a good or bad way. Mind what you say.

Wearing: Most of the time the clothes we wear are directly or indirectly influenced by the people around us and what may look appealing to us. Personally, I'm a big fan of wearing suits. I find that when I wear one, I naturally act and talk much more formally than when I would wear something more causal, such as a pair of basketball shorts and a T-shirt. Wearing something can subconsciously change the way you act and talk. I don't judge what people wear—it is entirely up to you—on a given day. In the long run, know that whatever you wear will shape your manners as a person.

Eat: Our body is like a car. If you don't change the oil in a car, check the radiator, or fail to put gas in the tank, your car will inevitably stop running. What you put inside your body is the same way. If you put in the wrong food or do stupid things to your body, it will inevitably affect you. Take care of your body because it's the only one you've got, and you can't replace it with a new one.

Have control of who you are around with, what you watch, what you say, what you hear, and what you eat.

If you hang out with chickens, you will cluck;
and if you hang out with eagles, you will fly.

—**Steve Maraboli**,
Unapologetically You: *Reflections on Life and the Human Experience*

TRAITS OF A GOOD FAMILY

Family cares for one another equally and loves each other dearly and unconditionally. A real family needs each other's love, time, company, forgiveness, patience and trust. A family naturally loves each other, but you must also understand the value of love and not destroy it.

A family must have time for one another—if you don't have time, which we highly doubt-- you must make time for them. Remember that the time you spend with them must be real and must have no interference, because it is family time. Treasure those moments. As you grow, time becomes more precious, and it will continue to diminish.

A family needs each other's company in desperate times and hardships. There will be tough times in your life that you or your loved ones can't overcome. That's when you or anyone in your family must shoulder the burden. If anyone in your family—including you, the reader—is having trouble, you must let your family know and let them help you. Don't keep any secrets from them.

There will be a day where you will get on each other's nerves. You must be patient because little fights can lead to lasting wounds. No one is perfect, and forgiveness is the ultimate solution.

The bond that links your true family is not one of blood, but of respect and joy in each other's life.

—Richard Bach

REVERSE CHECK-UP

We all know that parents check up on us and they always ask, "Have you done your homework?", "Have you done your chores?", and so on and forth. We can ask similar questions and keep parents on track. Simply asking our parents whether they have accomplished the tasks and goals they had for the day makes us informed and appreciative of what it takes to run a house and take care of a family.

Reverse checking will create opportunities for wonderful conversations and might as well be a window into the reality of life and responsibility. Be the first to ask, "Mom/Dad, how was your day?", "Were you able to accomplish your goals?", or "What do you have planned?"

Reverse every natural instinct and do the opposite of what you are inclined to do, and you will probably come very close to having a perfect golf swing.

—Ben Hogan

LEAVING A
LASTING IMPRESSION

The way you present yourself is how people will judge you. People judge other people unconsciously. Everyone judges one another unintentionally and intentionally. That explains the importance of leaving a good lasting impression on people you meet. It is especially important in a business environment. Your first impressions will become a vivid symbol of your personality and memory of who you are. Your first impressions will also determine how people will treat you and how they will associate with you.

Don't misunderstand what we are suggesting. We are not saying change who you are to make other people happy, because that is the very last thing you want to do for anyone. You are who you are, and you will change for the better over time and learn. And it is best not to try to behave in a way that isn't true to yourself.

Be yourself. Being yourself is the best way to represent yourself. That way, people who see you will then know the person with whom they're associating.

We are advocating for a fine presentation of yourself. Everyone likes a good presentation.

The fact that we are impressed by a fine presentation of a delicious dish doesn't affect its original flavor. Rather, it enhances its appeal.

Almost everyone will make a good impression,
but only a few will make a good lasting impression.

—**Sonya Parker**

ASK, THINK AND EXECUTE!

Asking for other people's opinions is a good idea. Blindly applying people's advice to your circumstances, however, is not advised.

Before you take someone else's opinion and go along with it, make sure you are 100% sure that you're making a good decision and think about whether it will help you. If you need someone's help with something, consult an expert on the subject. Go to people who have experienced similar situations and have seen the pros and cons of the problem or task you face. Once you are fully informed, you can make the best decision possible.

Be who you are and say what you feel because those who mind don't matter, and those who matter don't mind.

—Unknown [CA18]

SERVE

You don't have to get old to appreciate the value of service. Be kind, help others and be a force of positive energy. It feels great to help people when they are in need. Instead of sitting home isolated from the possibilities of interacting with the world around you, you are better off to be engaged with your community.

Yes, there are bad things out there, too, and it is much easier to be at home away from undesirable situations. However, we often forget that some of the best lessons of life come from observing circumstances that are outside of our comfort zone. An Afghan proverb says, "good lessons are the result of bad circumstances."

Help people, serve at any opportunity that comes your way, as that will become the source of our joy.

Let no one ever come to you without leaving better and happier. Be the living expression of God's kindness: kindness in your face, kindness in your eyes, kindness in your smile.

—Mother Teresa

THE DISTANCE BETWEEN SUCCESS AND FAILURE CAN BE HALF A MILE

The more you become independent, the more you must deal with temptations. These temptations include going out with friends, using your phone to watch something, playing on a console, and so on, instead of prioritizing essential tasks. These are not easy choices.

We have a huge family with grandparents, six uncles, six in-laws, 21 cousins, and one aunt. Most of them live within a two-mile radius. We meet every Friday, Saturday, and even occasionally on weekdays at my grandparents' house, a half-mile away from us.

In other words, a total distraction from our essential tasks and potential failure was essentially down the road. It was like there was a party we were invited to a few times a week. They would make fantastic food and delicious desserts, and we would all hang out, talk and argue for fun. As if this was not enough, we had friends texting us and wanting to hang out or to go downtown for a day trip. We were always facing temptations and had tough choices to make. We had a pretty regular choice of having fun with friends and family or balance the fun by focusing on our work.

We were still able to attend the gatherings, enjoy the company of an army of dynamic personalities, and eat delicious fatty food and irresistible desserts. Of course, we were not perfect, and there were times when we completely ignored our homework and preparation for finals. We found and took advantage of the opportunities of just having fun. This is when our parents would pull us back and remind us of our responsibilities. Sometimes, it took more than just gentle reminders.

We had friends who told us to go places with them for leisure. Had we done so, we would have sacrificed the things that have helped us in the long run, even potentially ruining our future success. At such a time, failure was only a phone call or text away. Even worse, sometimes, failure was standing right next to us, talking to us and trying to persuade us to have fun instead of doing what we had to do if we wanted to enjoy the success we were envisioning. It's hard, we know, but it sure as hell is worth it.

In life, those who give up their fun and time for the greater good of their future and the future of their loved ones is admired and cherished more.

Don't be afraid to give up the good to go for the great.

—John D. Rockefeller

STRUGGLES AND UNWANTED CIRCUMSTANCES

We have shared many examples of how one can better himself. We all must understand and remember that we will never be perfect and that every situation in our lives will not be ideal. What matters is that we strive for perfection, even in times of struggles or trying circumstances.

We must strive to keep bettering ourselves even when it's hard. It is a trait we assume to become a permanent part of our character.

I have seen my family and friends struggle. In each situation, the hardest thing for them to do was to keep moving forward, bettering themselves and looking forward to favorable circumstances. At times, we may get so caught up in the problem that we end up creating more issues for ourselves. There were times when my family brought up past mistakes and struggles that had nothing to do with us at the moment. As a result, there was a lack of thinking and calm assessment of the situation at hand.

Your present circumstances don't determine where you can go; they merely determine where you start,

– Nido Qubein

THE COLORS OF LIFE

When I was six years old and Imran was four, our dad became a diplomat in London, causing the family to move to England. During our summer breaks between school years, we traveled to many countries and experienced many different cultures and walks of life. While growing up there, I saw the differences and similarities of people in the U.S. compared to people in England.

People live in different parts of this planet and have many different lifestyles. They eat different foods, wear different clothes and celebrate different holidays. They have evolved differently than we have. Their experiences and circumstances are and have been different than our own. They speak different languages—and even when they speak the same language, they speak different dialects and have different pronunciations. They look different from me and you, and their skin color may be different from ours, too. Their beliefs and values may differ from ours. Despite all these differences, the striking thing for us was that expressions such as laughter or sadness where, universal languages.

Being conscious of one fundamental truth in life is paramount. A human from Africa or Asia or the Amazon jungle in Brazil are all equally human, and we must acknowledge and cherish our differences. Those who have been able to travel and interact with other people whose values, lifestyle and cultures differ from ours tend to be mindful of giving the same respect to other humans. We must not be judgmental because someone's appearance or set of circumstances is not like ours. Life has given us different colors: we must cherish the diversity of life, and we must be mindful of the opportunities for learning what we can from one another.

We must get out of our bubble, travel the world and learn new things. If you do, you will grow as a far more well-rounded person.

The truth is, I'll never know all there is to know about you just as you will never know all there is to know about me. Humans are by nature too complicated to be understood fully. So, we can choose either to approach our fellow human beings with suspicion or to approach them with an open mind, a dash of optimism and a great deal of candor.

—Tom Hanks

TIME/SCHEDULING

SCHEDULING

One of the mandatory elements of success is a method of scheduling your day. It can be in whatever way you prefer—whether it's writing it out in a planner or typing it into an electronic device. This helps you see what you're doing visually; and naturally, you will become more productive than if you were just going about your day with complete loss and confusion. As young adults, we had days where we would know in the back of our minds that there were things we had to do; but we would never get to them—because we either forgot or would just drift to something else. Why? Because we hadn't scheduled it as if it were something we had to do. By creating a schedule for your day, you are holding yourself accountable. Essentially, you are saying "these are my priorities, and I must do them." Here's an example of how someone might write down his or her list:

Must-Do List	To-Do List
Sleep at 9 p.m. and Wake Up at 6 a.m. (Alarm)	Homework
(6:15 a.m.) Drink a small cup of water, and exercise (30 min)	Help Mom with dishes
Shower, relax, & meditate (5 min)	Get ready for soccer
(7:15 a.m.) Eat breakfast	Organize closet
(7:45 a.m.) Go to school	Get ready for the game tomorrow

Above is an example of what we used to remind us of our priorities. It is what we call a to-do list and a must-do list. The must-do side is about consistent actions performed daily to stay on track. From that foundation, we go onto our priorities: the to-do list is always changing and adapting to our day. What is most important, what needs to be done soonest, goes at the top of that list, and so on.

Again, this is just an example of our way. It is entirely up to you how you should schedule out your day. The important thing is to do it daily.

Knowing is not enough; we must apply.
Being willing is not enough; we must do.

—Leonardo da Vinci

FINISH YOUR TO-DO LIST, OR IT WILL BECOME YOUR MUST-DO LIST

Over time, unfinished tasks that are part of your to-do list will become mandatory and end up what we label as your must-do list. Let's identify some examples of a to-do list and must-do list.

Completing your work/homework, eating, brushing teeth, and sleeping are some items on your must-do list.

Your to-do list items are things that you may not do daily in a routine way. This could include taking your brother to his doctor's appointment. So, your must-do list is rather an obligatory routine you practice. On the other hand, your to-do list could be a necessary part of your daily to-do list but things you must complete by a given time and/or within a certain set of requirements.

Now, let's say we didn't finish something on our to-do list. This unfulfilled task then moves to our must-do list, due to lack of time management, pure procrastination, or in the event of emergency situations. Whatever the reason may be, incomplete tasks will result in affecting the rest of your schedule and obligations.

I never used to schedule for anything. Instead, it was all last minute for me. Whether it was pulsed-based (ßwhat does pulsed-based mean?) plans with friends or rushing to doctor's appointments at the last second, I always found myself desperate to just catch up.

I wouldn't finish a specific task, and it would end up ruining my day. Sometimes, I would even give up on the rest of the tasks for the day because I thought that if I didn't complete one, it was useless trying to complete the others.

I came to my senses trying to figure out why I wasn't accustomed to scheduling, even though some of my peers did it with ease. Eventually, I got frustrated because I had created a bad trend. Every month, I'd try to go back to scheduling, and it would work for me the first week, but after that, I would find myself at square one again.

The mistake I was making is something a considerable number of people do, and they do it unknowingly even though it is obvious. Whenever I started to schedule, the first week was all glorified by check signs next to all my to-do and must-do items. It wasn't complicated. I knew what I had to do, and I'd do everything in my ability to get it done. Then, for one reason or, another I changed after the first week. Once the successful first week had passed, there was more of an "I know what to do, but I can do this later" attitude. Then, it became more of an "I can have fun now; I need not stress about these tasks" attitude. It was my lack of commitment to what I needed to do. It was also a lack of discipline. I didn't have a sense of urgency in what I needed to fulfill. Lots of young adults overlook this simple custom.

Don't let even the smallest things in your schedule become something that you can do "later on." Imran and I used to procrastinate, and there are times we still do. However, we have gotten better. When I got into the habit of writing down a schedule, most times I'd fulfill the task without worrying about time limits. We do our best, so our to-do list doesn't slide into our must-do list. In whatever way you schedule, do not let a task go; finish it.

Do the little things before they become the big things.

— Billy Cox

USING YOUR TIME PRODUCTIVELY TO BE FREE LATER ON

Many teens and young adults, ourselves included, leave their priorities and tasks untouched until the absolute last minute. Or, the time we have is just used in a way where it is wasted rather than used productively. This then causes many people to procrastinate; and instead of using the time productively and getting the tasks done, it is the complete opposite.

The time is wasted on pointless things that are very fulfilling and fun in the moment but at the last second cause lots of stress because there is barely any time to finish whatever priorities weren't attended to. There were times when Imran and I wouldn't even try to get our work done simply because we knew there was no point.

We didn't have the time to finish it. Then the stress would set in, and the work would pile up. In the end, it would take much more time and effort to catch up on the things we could have finished and gotten done easily.

A personal example of this would be when I was younger and had a project due for my eighth-grade final. I didn't check what the instructions were for the project and, to be honest, I didn't even care about it. I pushed it out of my mind anytime the thought of it came up. This later affected me negatively because of the constant stress. Neither you nor I can trick ourselves into forgetting something that we must complete or do.

Eventually, the essay crept up on me and gave me one of the worst days a student could have. Because of my lack of discipline to complete what I needed to do, it crept up on me slowly. I not only had to finish the eight-page essay, but also had other homework to complete that night. Fortunately, I completed everything, but I had to forego sleep. And because of the lack of sleep, the next day was disrupted.

It ruined how I learned and how I got things done for the day after. Either wasn't alone in my procrastination. I knew friends who would wait until Sunday night to do all of their homework for the next day or homework due at 11:59. Every single time I saw them the next morning for school, they were always tired and they had bags under their eyes, and I could tell they were slowly losing their hair because of lack of sleep.

When you finish your priorities first, you won't have work piling up on itself, and it won't hinder your other activities. Getting things done right away will become your habit. Remember, there is no need to rush, either. A coach once told me that slow is smooth and smooth is fast. If you learn to take things step by step, you can complete them a lot quicker than trying to finish everything at once. If you rush the work and don't do it properly, it will come back to haunt you.

So, we recommend that you get your work done, whatever that requires of you, and do it as soon as possible. Everything we do, or are required to do, takes time. By all means, if you are 100% sure, and you can do your work quickly, then go for it. Otherwise, be patient, take your time and get your work done so you can be free later on.

Don't be fooled by the calendar. There are only as many days in the year as you make use of. One man gets only a week's value out of a year, while another man gets a full year's value out of a week.

—**Charles Richards**

TIME IS VALUABLE, KNOW HOW TO USE IT

For the vast majority of people, accomplishing a productive and prosperous life takes an investment of time, effort, focus and discipline.

Young adults have the advantage of time compared to adults. We are blessed with extraordinary energy, and nature has gifted us a huge deposit of time. The flipside of a young adult's life is a lack of appreciation for time and a lack of focus on the things that will expedite our success. Using time productively is something that many young adults don't consider. Everything discussed on this subject will determine the value of our outcomes.

Life is full of all sorts of distractions. Keeping yourself on track and using your time as an investment in your future is the one sure way to rewarding outcomes.

Yesterday's the past, tomorrow's the future, but today is a gift. That is why it's called the present.

—Bill Keane

USING TIME WITH VALUE

For many people, even adults, times come when we have a bunch of free time and nothing to do. This happens a lot more with teens and young adults. You wake up and have the whole day to yourself without any responsibilities. I'm here to tell you that if you think you have nothing to do with your "free time," then I don't buy it. There are plenty of things to do in the free time you have, besides just having fun. Fun is the first thing that comes to mind because it's ... fun. It's enjoyable; you don't work for it; most often it's a click, a drive and a reach into your pocket away. What I am getting at is that the very time you have might be valuable to use for something else besides fun. I'm not implying to forego fun, do so and enjoy it, but use your time valuably.

What we're about to tell you isn't to make you feel depressed, but to help you out in the long run. You may be a boy or a girl, young or old, but at the end of the day, everyone will die. And as far as society knows, we have only one life. The choices you make and what you do with the time that you have will shape who you will become and what will become of your life. When you become older, you will think one of two things. You will either look back at your life and be filled with regret, or you will look back at your life and be 100% grateful that you didn't waste your chances.

You can either put value in whatever you do, or you can put none. Your time can either be your friend or your enemy. It's all about how you use it and how much you value and cherish it.

Time is more valuable than money.
You can get more money, but you cannot get more time.

—Jim Rohn

DOING THE RIGHT THING AT THE RIGHT TIME

Some people confuse the concept of "doing things on time" and "everything has its time." We are encouraged to do the right thing at the right time.Since a young age, we are told "that everything has its time" and "do everything in its time." To us, it didn't make sense, and it might not make sense to you. The right time comes, but doing the right thing in that moment of time is up to each individual. Sometimes, things will happen for you at the right time and place without you playing a role. We discussed how important it is to finish your tasks on time. However, as we grow, we learn the importance of the implications of what we say or do and knowing that everything has its time and place. The time could be now, years later, minutes ahead or it could have passed, and there is a new right time to achieve or say or do something. Just know that each time you are in that right moment, it will be used for one or more solid purposes. Bear in mind that you must spend that time effectively on the right project.

Everything has a time and place. Be aware of this, and you will not only accomplish more but also have more leisure than those who are always in a hurry.

—Tryon Edwards

REDEFINE TIME

While we have no control over the extension of time, we are capable of using time as we wish. The secret is redefining your time. I redefined my time by visualizing it.

In 10th grade, I was taking a Spanish class, and each day, I would go to the classroom and look at the clock. It was an involuntary habit I formed. When I looked at the time, I'd understand that I had an hour, and it was represented graphically and imprinted on my imagination. This made the one hour feel much longer. By visualizing time, you realize how much time you have left to complete a task. This way, you give time meaning and value.

By redefining your time, you do two things. First, time isn't controlling you anymore; you are controlling your own time. By looking at the time, you feel a sense of responsibility in completing tasks and things beneficial to you. Secondly, you can visualize your whole day and get a sense of what you will do with the remaining hours.

Start redefining your time, so you can redefine your life.

You don't get paid for the hour. You get paid for the value you bring to the hour.

—Jim Rohn

DON'T LET THE PURSUIT OF PERFECTION STOP YOU FROM COMPLETING TIME-SENSITIVE TASKS

Most of us are programmed to having it our way, the "perfect" way, or the best way possible. Often, the "perfect" way or our way is unnecessary, sometimes it's not even the correct or the objectively "perfect" way.

Our knowledge may be limited and therefore our understanding about getting something done "perfectly," or having it entirely our way may be imperfect or not meeting requirements. Regardless, not having it your way or the "perfect" way must not stop you from finishing your tasks.

My brother and I have a close friend who always pursued perfection to the point where he never achieved successes. He would always insist upon the most fun or the best way to spend his time. Otherwise, there would be no fun at all.

Spending his time the best way possible is something to admire—he appreciates his time—but, you can't let the pursuit of perfection stop you from pursuing what you want. Take the opportunities presented to you and use them the best you can.

Do not allow the pursuit of perfection to undermine the opportunity itself.

**Things may come to those who wait,
but only the things left by those who hustle.**

—Abraham Lincoln

SMALL STEPS

There are people with legitimate limitations of all kinds. On the other hand, many people have reasons they can't succeed, blaming their circumstances for "not having enough" or thinking it's because they don't have enough help.

Small steps fueled by passion and perseverance will help overcome many hurdles. Eventually more opportunities will open up, resources will be identified, and people will offer help.

I am reading a book about Winston Churchill and his life. It was intimidating to read a book of this size. My dad gave me a technique he used when he would read a book. It's simple, and I'm sure many people already do this. He told me to cut the book in small sections of about 10, 20, or even 30 pages. He used the "Simplify Complexities" technique which we will talk about in the next chapter. Each day you finish, let's say ten pages. Ten pages a day isn't much; by the end of the month, you would have read the entire book. It's all about how you see your goal and how you go about accomplishing it. You can do this with all major tasks that may seem impossible at first.

Hewad never wanted to start anything because he was holding out for the perfect situation to begin the work. I, on the other hand, was able to practice my soccer in a small living room with the help of no one. It wasn't just my passion and my determination, but also my lack of concern for things I didn't have. I focused on what we did have. Even when I had nothing, I would still pursue my goals. I taught Hewad something that he now uses and will always use for the rest of his life: The first small steps you achieve in anything, make the biggest differences for you.

The journey of a thousand miles begins with one step.

—Lao Tzu

INVEST ONE HOUR A DAY

Our dad read an article called "The Value of One Hour." The article explained that if you invest one hour a day to a certain thing with no distractions, you will become very good at it.

A typical college class runs ten weeks or a quarter. Let's say the course is about the Egyptian pyramids and their history in the context of the period in which they were built.

A professor will teach this one hour a day, four times a week. By the end of the tenth week—a typical college quarter—you would have studied this subject and learned all they could teach you in 40 hours of uninterrupted and fully dedicated time.

Let's say you decide to take two more quarters of the academic year on the same subject, and then decide to not take a break and to study the same subject during the summer quarter. By the end of the entire year, you would have invested 80 hours in learning about ancient Egyptian pyramids.

By investing one hour of your time, uninterrupted and fully dedicated to the research and study of the ancient Egyptian pyramids, by the end of the year, you would have studied this subject for 272 hours that year. This could be any subject, sport, skill, or anything you want to learn.

One hour per day of study in your chosen field is all it takes. One hour per day of study will put you at the top of your field within three years. Within five years, you'll be a national authority. In seven years, you can be one of the best people in the world at what you do.

—**Earl Nightingale**

PLAN/KNOW WHAT YOU WANT TO DO EARLY

Our natural instincts fuel our desire to excel in our personal lives and career. Nearly everyone is out and about pursuing something he/she wants or needs. We always see people—including ourselves—not planning on how they will get what they want or need.

This could be in their career or buying a new car, or other areas. Nearly everything requires planning. The people who know what they want plan on how to get what they want ... and most often, those are the people who do get it or are successful.

I have yet to figure out what major I want to pursue in college. To this day, I still don't know what's best for me, and that's the truth. But I am still looking, and while I look, I learn new things, and I go through many experiences. Plus, I have some ideas of what I am looking forward to doing.

You can discover what you want to do early on by putting yourself in different situations or by trying to do a certain thing; if it doesn't work, move on. If it did, then keep looking into it. My mom forced me into so many things! And although I didn't like most of those things, her efforts made it easier for me to figure out what I did like.

If you are failing to plan, you are planning to fail.

—Tariq Siddique

HAVE A PLAN

The older you grow, the more you will realize how competitive our world is. There are people striving to get a job, passionately working to get a raise or better income, and students working hard to be the best in class. Therefore, it is necessary to know two things: you must know what you want to become early on, and what will make you special or unique in that pursuit. Failing that, you will join the ever-increasing population trying to just survive, get by, and at best maintain the status quo.

Humans are capable of reaching extraordinary accomplishments. No extraordinary accomplishment has ever happened without a precise plan and a persistent pursuit of it.

A goal without a plan is just a wish.

—Unknown

HAVE A PLAN B

I know people who have worked toward something for years, and then sadly that dream they had didn't come true. They were stuck—they didn't know where to go or what to do. Thinking they would succeed, they ended up losing it all. Most of the time, the goal or dream is hard but possible to achieve. Either they hadn't evaluated their methods, or they lacked a plan B. We saw this show where this hard-working, fairly old couple worked on an invention for eight years. Eight years.

They both put everything they had into it thinking they would make it, and they didn't. Since they didn't have a backup plan, they were shocked and didn't know what to do next. Life can bear these unpleasant outcomes. Maybe the goal you intended to achieve was a great objective, but the plan was terrible. You must spread out your options and be open-minded and flexible in examining your plans and ways of pursuing your goal.

Remember, don't focus too much on plan B; just make sure it's there. We are used to letting things that aren't as important as our initial plans get in the way. In the end, our focus becomes divided into two, and neither work out as we envisioned.

A friend of Hewad told him not to focus on two sports at once. When Hewad was 12, he wanted to play both basketball and soccer. Even though Hewad was good at both sports, the pressure of time and school work ended up forcing him to choose only one.

Plan B is just that; Plan B. It is there for when, and if at all, necessary. While you're creating your Plan B, think of every scenario where things can go wrong and make your Plan B immune to those problems you think likely to occur with Plan A. When your Plan B is created, you put it aside. You go on and pursue your initial plan, and think of every possible scenario and shortcoming you can address now. If and when things go wrong, that's when you start implementing Plan B. Your plan B should be a back-up to your Plan A.

**If a plan didn't work, don't worry, the alphabet
has 25 more letters.**

—Unknown

COMPLACENCY IS YOUR ENEMY

According to the Cambridge Dictionary, complacent means, "feeling so satisfied with your abilities or situation that you feel you do not need to try any harder." There are two things I want to get at with this topic, and two kinds of people I want to address. These are the two people I notice most, and I was also both kinds.

The first kind have a complacent mentality. It is just who they are. They are just normal people like you and me. It isn't bad to have a normal, ordinary life, but being complacent has a big downside to it. These people go to school, and they come back, they may be doing other activities outside of school. Other than that, they have their devices, and they have friends who are on the same wavelength. They have a routine schedule and activities, and as such, they are not open to new experiences.

Because of this repetitive routine, they end up having too much spare time on their hands. We humans must keep ourselves busy with things, so our mind doesn't get the best of us. The reason young students and teens are so stressed is that they don't want to put effort into doing more with their life. Their thinking and their mentality don't go beyond their own home. Complacency drains motivation; it's a matter of self-discipline and choice to get past it.

The second kind of person I notice are the ones who go the extra mile, but stop right when they have reached whatever extra goal or achievement they wanted. As soon as they reach it, they don't create a new goal for themselves and they don't raise the bar because, to them, they have reached their goal. Hewad had the talent to do whatever he wanted because he truly could excel in all the things he put his mind to. Unfortunately, his narrow-minded thinking and his complacency was like a huge iron ball attached to his leg with a chain, preventing him from reaching his potential. Sometimes, he would get past that complacency and those were the only times where he would excel. Everyone (besides his family) could tell he had hidden potential in many things, but his complacency was preventing him from further progress.

Those who are chained to a psychological iron ball can, and must, free themselves. Every one of us has the potential to achieve more if we overcome complacency.

Of all the possible avenues of life there are to live for, complacency should be viewed as the switch that killed the will to build.

—Gillis Triplett

DON'T LEAVE ANYTHING TO CHANCE

I watched a movie a while back called "Heat." It was a phenomenal movie, and it taught me a few things. The villain, played by Robert De Niro, left nothing to chance. He would pay attention to every detail of what he had to do, and he would do the job flawlessly. He wouldn't let the small things turn into bigger hurdles. He wouldn't do anything halfway nor do some parts better than the others. Everything he did was with full attention and focus, so nothing was left to become a bigger problem. That's what made him such an accomplished villain in the movie.

Often, people are motivated to achieve a task, but, at the final push toward completion, impatience hits, and the person does just half of the job. As a result, all the time and effort they invested into the project goes to waste. Still the task remains undone, and they will likely have to deal with it again at some point in the future.

Imagine the times you could have prevented something by doing a little extra work or research. There may have been many situations where a little more effort and better focus could have prevented whatever bad circumstance or issue you ended up facing.

You aren't alone; this happens to nearly everyone. Even to the best of us this sort of thing happens.

Don't leave anything to chance and complete the task at hand. Otherwise you subconsciously adopt a bad habit.

I don't believe in luck. Luck equals leaving things to chance and the outside world. I believe in being harbingers of our fate, determining our path, taking action and creating our destiny in life.

"This is your life, and it is yours to create.
Don't let others do it for you."

—Unknown

LEARN TO EVALUATE

Sometimes, we find ourselves in unpleasant and challenging circumstances. Circumstances--good and bad-- will inevitably occur to or near a person. Some you can see coming. Others you can't, and you wouldn't be able to predict. We might witness a situation, at one time, while elsewhere we are a part of another. For example, when making important choices that will result in inevitable effects on us, such as applying for college, buying a house, moving somewhere new or changing jobs, we must have the ability to evaluate the circumstances and choose discriminately based on the facts, the pros and the cons. Often, even when the circumstance is time sensitive, it is both possible and positive to step back, evaluate and then decide. If you can't decide, seek help. Start a conversation with your parents or close friends and family. Share with them your ideas, concerns and yes, if you have them, tell them about your fears.

Although rare, you may encounter the urge of thinking fast. You will be able to see through a complex task and determine your options. Everything you evaluate and the course of action you take will seem to have come naturally. Even you may be impressed by the promptness of your accurate reaction in a time-congested situation. However, this is not your license to deal with every last-minute situation. Nor does it give you the universal knowledge and ability to overcome every time-constrained task. Many times I have regretted my decisions because I didn't take time to step back and evaluate my choices.

You will find yourself among friends in situations that are either productive or just straight up fun. Participating in such gatherings is a good use of time. On the flip side, sometimes, the same friends may be doing something unhealthy or illegal; it is vital to not take part in such situations. We don't want to sound like your mom or dad, but it's important not to ruin your life by making snap decisions. Trust us. We know close friends and family that have screwed up their whole lives from "being in the moment." They shouldn't have put themselves in that situation in the first place!

Life is much more than just being in the moment. So, don't ruin your life over one dumb thing. Ask yourself "is this worth my health?" Questions like this will steer you away from potential trouble.

So, learn to evaluate circumstances instantaneously. If you find a circumstance either fun, educational or productive, participate. If there is an issue, address it, and deal with it in the best way possible. Fortunately, the world offers great alternatives, and you have the choice to avoid the negatives.

**Take a step back, evaluate what is important,
and enjoy life.**

—Teri Garr

HAVE FUN ...
BUT BE MODERATE

Too much of just about anything is, well, not fun and can even be detrimental. Moderation is the ultimate balance between competing forces around you. Moderation harmonizes your way through good and bad times.

While temptations and peer pressure will push you away from your priorities, moderation helps you regain your focus.

To this day, it is not fun recalling the countless hours Imran and I spent playing video games. We vividly remember that our fun just became repetitive and ultimately, utterly boring. At the time, we had one good friend who had mastered both self-discipline and moderation. He would put his priorities in front of anything else and have genuine fun time afterwards. I could tell that he appreciated every moment of free time he had. We highly advocate moderation and knowing when to do what.

**If one oversteps the bounds of moderation, the greatest
pleasures cease to please.**

—Epictetus

COMMITTING AND ASSUMING BEFORE CHECKING

Do you recall committing to something only to realize moments later that you aren't able to fulfill your end of the bargain? We do. I'll give you an example.

A friend asked me to go with him to the beach. Right away I told him I was able to go, even though, I wasn't sure. So, I asked my dad if I was able to go to the beach with him. My dad reminded me of my urgent priorities and said no. Reluctantly, I called and told my friend I couldn't go.

That didn't seem like a big deal, but now, my friend had to change his plans, and I also had put myself in the bad situation of having to explain myself. This was a self-created and self-imposed situation. Alternatively, I could have told my friend that I would first check with my dad. This way, my friend wouldn't have had to change his plans twice.

Before you commit to any agreement or plan, make sure you understand what the requirements of you are and make sure that you are available and capable of fulfilling your commitment. That's simple, yet it goes right over many people's heads when they are in the moment. Don't commit before you check; check before you commit.

When you make an assumption, you are preparing the room for error.

—Toba Beta,
My Ancestor Was an Ancient Astronaut

ACTIONS

PEOPLE CONFUSE FUN WITH SATISFACTION

Face Reality, Change the Reality → It's hard to face facts, especially if there a lot of difficulties that life has thrown your way. In times like that, it's even easier to run away from reality by having fun and never dealing with it, even though we know it's there.

What we forget is that we will deal with a problem eventually or now. You will never change your reality and solve the problems you avoid facing. Although, it's hard to do, you must.

Facing your reality is the first step, and the next step is to change it. Whenever I was unhappy with the way things were going, or I didn't like an outcome of a certain situation, most often, I would do nothing about it, and let it slide. This became a bad habit that took a while to break. I found myself much happier when I dealt with a problematic situation right away. It wasn't always easy, but it was much better to be relieved of the stress than to have to worry constantly.

Changing the reality is best to do on your terms however it suits you, but in a way, that's beneficial for your future. A good friend that I've known for about five years is very distant now. This is not because he has ill will toward anyone. He wanted to change his reality, to change his life. He was always very keen on going out with people, having fun, and living the good life, but he found that he was never satisfied. He always told me he was happy about his life. He always had fun, and there was nothing to complain about—yet, he never felt satisfied. I told him it was just human nature never to be satisfied. He thought that was a lie and said there are many people he knew who were very satisfied with their lives, and still happy at the same time. After about a year of not seeing this friend, he called me one day and wanted to catch up. He offered to pick me up, and I agreed.

After catching up with him on the way to his house, we talked about my life and what I was up to. I said that things were going well and that I had nothing to complain about. Then, he asked me if I was satisfied with how things were going and, truthfully, I told him that, some days, I was very satisfied with myself. I asked him why he was being so distant and isolating himself, and he said, "I completely changed my life around, I stopped hanging out with a lot of people, stopped doing things just for fun, and started to spend time with family." I asked why he did this, and he explained that he had been happy with his life, but the lack of satisfaction slowly turned his happiness into unhappiness and depression. For a while, he kept doing the same things. Then one day he woke up and said to himself that the way things were going wasn't how he wanted to live. So, he stopped hanging out with friends, wasting time and just having fun with no purpose. By changing his routine, he discovered why he was never satisfied, and the reason was that although he had fun and a great life, there had been no purpose to his everyday activities. By figuring this out, he not only found a purpose, but he also became much more disciplined and more productive. After telling me all this, I asked him jokingly, "Are you satisfied?" He answered with a big grin, "Yes." He understood that something was wrong, and he changed it for himself.

> So many people live within unhappy circumstances and yet will not take the initiative to change their situation because they are conditioned to a life of security, conformity, and conservation, all of which may appear to give one peace of mind, but in reality, nothing is more damaging to the adventurous spirit.

> — **Christopher McCandless**

COMMUNICATE EFFECTIVELY

Communicate things you want, desire, or need in a clear, effective way. You will be communicating all throughout your life in unfamiliar environments and with many types of people from various backgrounds. It is important to get your point across when you must, not in a whiny, childish way but effectively, assertively, and yet in a calm, collected and respectful manner.

Mature and educated people won't gravitate to someone who is loud, ignorant, or can't properly describe what he or she wants. One would rather hear a kid ask for candy than a kid who shouts and cries before he says he wants candy. Fortunately, we can learn and master effective communication by practicing it in our daily interactions with other people.

Former President Barack Obama didn't become president solely for his political ability, but in large part due to how well he communicated his vision for the country. He did it with kindness and charisma. My dad mentions the likes of Martin Luther King Jr., Malcolm X, and Bill Clinton as leaders with tremendous communication skills. Their communication skills are admired by many people.

As young adults, we must learn when to be blunt and when to be silent. We must learn and observe. We must know when to be passionate and smart. It all depends on the circumstances, and your audience. No matter who you talk with, you should have confidence in yourself and always be yourself, because the most likable people are the ones who are the most authentic.

Take advantage of every opportunity to practice your communication skills so that when important occasions arise, you will have the gift, the style, the sharpness, the clarity, and the emotions to affect other people.

— Jim Rohn

GET OUT OF YOUR COMFORT ZONE

There's a point in our lives when we hit the final versions of ourselves: Death. Again, we don't want you to feel depressed by this or saddened. Instead, we encourage you to be more motivated before you, ultimately, expire.

A lack of motivation at some point of our life makes us confined to our own houses and rooms and in front of television or computer screens - we become closed-minded to learning about new and different things.

School is one example of learning, but self-investment and self-education is another example. Many people don't put the effort and time into doing anything other than their daily must-do activities. There are billions of people on the earth doing what you do: wake up—if they are lucky enough—shower, eat, go to work or school, come home, do homework or spend time with their families, eat, sleep, and repeat the cycle.

So, if that lifestyle suits you and if you're happy with it, then continue. To each his own. On the other hand, most of us want to progress and do more with our time and given abilities.

Most who live in the developed countries have the opportunities billions of our fellow humans can't even imagine being a living reality. We live in places that are peaceful and rich with great infrastructure and services, making our lives ever more comfortable. Yet some people are unhappy, unsatisfied and unhealthy.

Not having the courage to challenge ourselves and serve greater causes than our own routine needs and desires is, at best, stagnation. It may be the safest yet the most damaging place to inhabit permanently.

> Be willing to step outside your comfort zone once in a while; take the risks in life that seem worth taking. The ride might not be as predictable if you'd just planted your feet and stayed put, but it will be a heck of a lot more interesting.
>
> — Edward Whitacre, Jr.

EXCELLING BEYOND THIS POINT

We fail to realize there are many better things behind our comfort zone and above whatever obstacles we face. If we are too lazy and too scared, we will never know, nor will ever realize our potential. Unless, of course, we truly try.

The comfort you so cherish and desperately hold onto now is less than the one you will feel after excelling beyond this point.

So, learn, grow, and shine above and beyond.

The limits of the possible can only be defined by going beyond them into the impossible.

— Arthur C. Clarke

TAKING CARE OF
YOURSELF PHYSICALLY

If you look good, you feel good. You're more confident, and you reflect onto others a sense of maturity and attractiveness. Taking care of your body not only makes you healthier, but it makes you disciplined.

We play soccer. It's a sport we grew up with throughout our lives. We are very passionate about it and get very serious when playing it. At this year's tryouts, Hewad got injured in his calf area, but, luckily, it was nothing serious. He was outraged because he knew that for two weeks he wouldn't be getting better at the game and instead would be getting worse. After his two weeks of recovery, he chose not to play for another two weeks as he became complacent and just lazy. Even though he played some pickup basketball and volleyball, he gained 20 pounds. He got worse at soccer, and he lost some of his confidence in the sport. This was because he wasn't playing to his full potential.

Through hard work he bounced back by doing extra training with me. He also cut the constant eating of unhealthy food. The way he accomplished this was whenever our parents would shop, he would make a list of things he needed and also things he didn't want. That way he would have no junk food around him, and there was no temptation to eat even a small bite.

Bouncing back and regaining your health is good. It's even better if you don't get yourself into the situation of having to bounce back. Sooner or later -- and more as you get older -- it will be harder to bounce back from gaining weight. Do whatever you must do to keep yourself in shape so there is no need to go through the struggles of losing weight.

In your schedule, make a set time to do some sort of activity, whether it's running, walking, push-ups, or whatever you would like to do. Make sure that you keep yourself fit. It's essential in young people's lives to keep themselves fit so they can live healthy and energetic lives.

Be miserable or motivate yourself. Whatever has to be done, it's always your choice.

—Wayne Dyer

IT'S ALL IN YOUR DELIVERY

Communication is a key part of a person's life. As noticed in earlier topics, it is a skill you can acquire and use. The tone and style of our communication is what truly changes the value of the message we convey to another person.

We often get into arguments with family members more than anyone else. Sometimes, we argue with friends or possibly people we barely know. A normal conversation slowly escalates and then reaches an argumentative state. Usually, this is when two people have opposing ideas. One person gets angry that the other person doesn't agree, and slowly but surely, the conversation turns into a large issue.

The best way to reach someone and the best way to get people to understand your viewpoint is to talk respectfully and sincerely. If you master these two things, you can and will win most people over to understand your viewpoint. Even when they disagree, the way you make the other person feel is what matters. If you try to talk to them from an attacking standpoint, they will attack back. Whenever you raise your voice, the other person will raise theirs. Whatever you do, the other person will mimic you. Whatever you deliver, you will receive back.

This is an important fact to understand, not only from a communication standpoint but in life, overall. There will be many circumstances when you must say things in a rather clever manner. Remember, people remember how you made them feel more than anything. You always have to watch how you talk. Your attitude and the way you speak will set the outcome of the other person's view of the situation and their response to it. The way you deliver is the way you will receive.

Your smile is your logo, your personality is your business card, how you leave others feeling after having an experience with you becomes your trademark.

—Unknown

VENT OUT NEGATIVE ENERGY POSITIVELY

We are susceptible to change, and we experience growth. As we grow, we are not familiar with the new things we experience right away. This shows that we are more vulnerable to failure. Therefore, we react to the changes unfamiliar to us and our reactions lack consistency. Our reactions, too, are the causes of the failures we experience. However, we can agree that our adjustment to these changes inflicts pressure on us, and as a result, some of us often feel stressed. Whatever kind of failure or shortcoming may be causing it, there's frustration that builds up. Bottling up your negative energy inside is not healthy. It is harmful to your body and mind. It wouldn't be normal if we didn't feel a little stressed or even upset at times, would it?

So, we must discuss and suggest ways to vent out the stress, anger and negativity. My brother and I barely ever wondered how our dad always stayed happy and positive. We would normally always be around my dad at soccer tournaments or home, and he would be watching us most of the time unless he got a phone call.

One day, I was on a soccer field, and I had just gotten done with my game. When I was done with soccer, I walked back with

Imran, and from afar, we saw this man, yelling and shouting. I was like, "Damn, Imran, look at this guy." As we were laughing, this guy stopped and walked toward us.

Then, as he got closer, I recognized him. Then I say to Imran, "Imran, you won't believe it man, but it's Dad" - and at this point, Imran's about to piss his pants - "That's Dad!" Imran's like, "No way, bro, impossible." "No really, it's him." Finally, after the confusion, our dad told us why he was shouting. He explained, "as a father who has a lot to do and think about, I sometimes feel pressure. Since I don't want to release any negativity onto my kids and wife, when I'm alone in the car or when I'm outside in a fairly deserted area, I unleash it by yelling."

We're not suggesting that you vent out the negativity as our dad does, but vent it out in such a way that doesn't affect other people. The fundamental lesson; don't vent your frustrations at the cost of others around you.

Some people don't even allow the negativity to affect them. Walking, running and being outside are ways of releasing negativity in a positive manner and the best defense against it. Clear your mind, and take care of your life through priorities - and if need be, vent out negative energy positively.

Suffering is traumatic and awful, and we get angry, and we shake our fists at the heavens, and we vent and rage and weep. But, in the process, we discover a new tomorrow, one we would never have imagined otherwise.

—Rob Bell

PROGRESS TO THE NEXT LEVEL OR SINK TO THE BOTTOM

Some young adults are constantly trying to move forward. It's important to better yourself, do your best and make progress at what will make your future brighter, better and more comfortable.

There is no alternative. As of 2018, there are seven and a half billion people living on our planet, and the vast majority of them are trying to survive.

The people that stand out are the ones that not only progress but also excel. Everyone admires these people and appreciates their hard work. They are ordinary men and women, but they get things done. They don't waste their time.

They don't get distracted and are great at avoiding temptations and short-sighted rewards. While everyone else is relaxing, they are working and bettering themselves every day.

Once they achieve their goals, they set even higher goals. They eventually end up serving greater causes, fighting disease and conquering new frontiers.

Set a higher goal for yourself, go get better and greater at something that is useful to others.

While you're out partying, horsing around, someone out there at the same time is working hard. Someone is getting smarter, and someone is winning.

Just remember that.

—Arnold Schwarzenegger

LOOK FOR
YOUR OPPORTUNITIES

It is ironic but true. To some of us, opportunities are like shooting stars: you hope, and you wish, and you pray for one to appear, but by the time one finally shows up, so much time has passed already. Either you can sit and wait for opportunities to come along or you can create your own until the massive ones come along. People forget that the big opportunity they were so patiently waiting for didn't come by chance or luck: your actions lead to the creation of that opportunity.

For many, it is much easier to sit in the spot we occupy right now and wait instead of creating opportunities for ourselves. People talk boastfully about how they will use the opportunity when it materializes. If and by the time that opportunity appears, the chances of us achieving that goal might have decreased due to other factors.

A big problem for me is the ability to start a task. It will take me a great deal of time before I actually get to it. By then, other distractions have cluttered my drive and motives. I would already be distracted by the simplest of things. So, I had to learn to create an opportunity and environment where I have no reason to avoid working. For this book, for example, I would find the quietest spot in the library and do my work. Previously I used to wait for the "perfect time" to start and no perfect time would ever appear.

The most successful people I have seen so far in my 16 years of living don't wait, but instead, take action and make opportunities for themselves. They don't let others dictate their lifestyle or situation; they create one for themselves. Those are the people that achieve success early in their life.

Opportunities are like sunrises. If you wait too long, you miss them.

—William Arthur Ward

FACE YOUR PROBLEMS AND FEARS HEAD-ON

I used to avoid homework, scheduling tasks and making appointments. I feared living the reality and still do at times. I was scared I wouldn't make it in life, and I was scared that I wouldn't become an accomplished person. I would think of all this instead of tackling the tasks before me. I would just consume an enormous amount of time thinking. I worried and stressed, and that did me no good. Nor will it do any good for you.

What a waste. I look back and know that all the stress was self-created due to my inaction. Like the friend I was talking about earlier, there came a day when I was fed up with how things were going for me. I took a total break from everyone and everything and just focused on how to change my ways of thinking and living. I learned to deal with a task right away. I was no longer leaving things to chance. I became more consistent. Deal with tasks right away and get them done. No one can force you to do your work, and most people wouldn't even care. Ultimately, it is your choice to do what you must.

**Running away from your problems is a race
you will never win.**

—Unknown

BE PREPARED AND
DO YOUR HOMEWORK

A small number of young adults are overachievers. We are not referring just to school work. These people put countless hours into researching and learning new skills and useful information. They do it out of genuine passion and/or for the enormous value they receive from their efforts.

A great example of this can be Kobe Bryant, LeBron James, or any other great sports athlete. Go to YouTube, search for their training regimens and look at how much time they invest into practicing new skills and tricks. These athletes study their opponents and their weaknesses and learn ways to make themselves more successful than their opponents. This takes time and effort. It doesn't fall from the sky.

Success is where preparation and opportunity meet.

— Bobby Unser

WITHOUT CONSISTENCY, THERE IS NO RESULT

You might be a smart, driven, talented, athletic, and even a genius with a great plan, but accomplishing your goals and completing tasks will require consistent focus and effort.

By now you can guess that I am the brother who, in addition to a number of useless habits, lacked persistence, focus and consistency. Many people told me I was a talented individual. People made comments saying I had the guts and passion and my future was bright. Something they didn't know about me that I knew was my profound procrastination and lack of persistence.

This book you are reading is a result of about three years of work. Yes; it is a long time, but it wasn't easy to gather the facts, research relevant quotes, learn how to publish, and too much more to describe. We gave up countless nights of going out with friends and attending fun family gatherings. Any noticeable imperfection is contrary to our aim. We have given our hearts to this book.

It is equally true that there were days that we could have dedicated to this project and would have it ready sooner, but we didn't. We simply lacked consistency and focus. Sometimes, there was a lack of drive, focus, persistence and commitment. Other times, we'd have our phones next to us and exchanged texts with people we have long forgotten.

Finally, we had to give it all up. We stopped texting people altogether, and we mean everyone. Until then, we barely got anything done. Why? We weren't being focused or consistent with what we were trying to achieve.

> "Success is neither magical or mysterious. Success is the natural consequence of consistently applying fundamentals."
>
> — **Jim Rohn**

ONE TASK AT A TIME

Usually, events unfold slowly over a period of time. As such, we should tackle tasks and fulfill our dues (ßdues?) step by step. This way, we avoid the possibility of being overwhelmed by dealing with much bigger loads of work all at once.

Many people try to multitask but do not realize that not every human is a woman and not every woman is a mother. We know of many men—including myself and my brother—who have tried to multitask and failed miserably. When you start many tasks at once and try to finish them all at once, there is a great probability that either most won't be accomplished, or none will be done well.

Whenever I started more than one task, my work was not as well-executed as it could have been. If multi-tasking has worked for you and you do it well, then keep doing so—but if you're like me, then it's best to keep your tasks separated by priority.

Start the tasks that are the most important and are due sooner. Get to them and only move to the next task after that and finish them one at a time. Do not let your mind go to pieces. I purposely repeat, I was a procrastinator.

Sometimes I would be in class doing my homework while the teacher was teaching a new topic. I would therefore miss the lesson and end up having trouble doing the related homework due next class. One time, when I knew I couldn't finish the homework, I distracted my math teacher by starting a conversation. (Sorry, Demona!) I was doing my homework while speaking to her. Don't ever get yourself in a position where you must do many tasks at once, but if do, make sure you finish one thing at a time. If necessary, get some help from others.

Since our dad was often on business trips, our mom paid the bills, managed our school, activities and the family's schedules. We were fortunate to be living near our cousins, uncles, aunts and grandparents. In addition to her responsibilities, our mom often received calls and texts from all her siblings and in-laws sharing their frustrations. Mom always did one thing at a time and people would praise her consistency, patience and perseverance. Had she allowed her mind to wander, she wouldn't have done the work so well, and no one would have praised her. She would rarely cook dishes that were not delicious. When she did, she was on the phone with her family. We could taste the difference.

Her cooking would turn out far more delightful and tasty when she wasn't distracted by the phone calls.

Concentrate all your thoughts upon the work at hand. The sun's rays do not burn until brought to a focus.

—Alexander Graham Bell

REPEATED ACTIONS

One of the great secrets of high achievers is that success is incredibly easy. Success is every bit as simple and (almost) as easy as failure, and you only need two little secrets.

The secret to success: A few easy daily habits.

The secret to failure: A few small mistakes every day.

That's it.

> Take up one idea. Make that one idea your life—think of it, dream of it, live on that idea. Let the brain, muscles, nerves, every part of your body, be full of that idea, and just leave every other idea alone. This is the way to success.
>
> —Swami Vivekananda

SIMPLIFY COMPLEXITIES AND BREAK DOWN ENORMOUS TASKS

Life is like a huge puzzle. This puzzle has big and tiny pieces. Often, we have small tasks and routines to take care of in a day, a week or a month. Other times, these small tasks and routines are part of a much bigger goal. For example, going to school every day of the week is a small but consistent routine that leads to college, a career and unimagined possibilities in life.

Occasionally, people will face "What the ****?" moments. This happens when a teen is given, for example, a 450-page book to read in six weeks and must then write a report and present it to the class.

The solution is to simplify complexities and subdivide enormous tasks. It's a rather simple concept. All you need to do is to take a huge project or goal and divide it into small chunks. Then, you work on whatever it is every single day until you accomplish the goal. Some tasks are harder to complete than others.

Let's stick with the 450-page book example. First, you would need to simplify the complexity by just focusing on the number of chapters in the book. By focusing on chapters, psychologically, you would have minimized the problem by a huge margin. Then, you would need to subdivide the enormous task by dividing 450 pages into 42 days because that is the number of days that comprise six weeks. Your result is 10.71 pages per day.

Example: 450-page book/42 days (six weeks) = 10.71 pages/ day.

This means the curveball that was thrown at you has now been changed into a consistent plan. Again, it will be harder to do with greater tasks or goals, but if you stick to this way of doing things, you will achieve things smoother than if done all at once. Think: rovers don't just end up on Mars's surface in one day.

**Out of the intense complexities,
intense simplicities emerge.**

—Winston Churchill

HOW YOU FACE
YOUR CIRCUMSTANCES

You will face many circumstances: happy, joyful, sad, harsh and painful. Everyone knows how to face a happy and joyful circumstance because it's easy. Many people don't know how to face a sad, harsh or painful circumstance. The same boiling water that softens a potato hardens the egg.

What matters is what you are made of, not the circumstances. However, we cannot entirely discount circumstances. Circumstances are opportunities for learning, becoming better, being at our best, and getting closer with family and friends. But essentially, it is the mindset and approach to life that are the determining factors. How desperately you desire a certain outcome will make the best of the circumstances you are facing.

When faced with a difficult circumstance, it is natural to feel stressed out or depressed, but what is essential is that we face it, overcome it, and persevere through it. You will be a much stronger person.

Running away from it will only make things worse. That circumstance isn't going away unless you do something about it.

Yes, sometimes friends or family may come in handy.

You must take personal responsibility. You cannot change the circumstances, the seasons, or the wind, but you can change yourself. That is something you have charge of.

—Jim Rohn

JUST START

When you look at a high-rise building, what do you see? You notice its height and the beauty of its structure and design. Let's look at Burj Khalifa, the tallest high-rise building in the world. If you look at it, the first thing you see is the height and beautiful structure. Then you realize how big the base of the building is compared to the top. The base and foundation of the building are just as important as the height.

Success is the same way. Starting out is one of the hardest parts of achieving what you want, but if it's not done, you might as well just stop dreaming about success. period.

We've all seen people talk about starting a new business or app, but as the saying goes, actions speak louder than words. You must start with your passionate desire and the resources you have available. Overtime, further resources, helping hands, and results will start trickling down.

The first step you take in achieving your goal is laying the foundation, just like the base of that building—without it, you cannot build or achieve anything. That is why it is important for you to have the courage to start; after that, you must have persistence, and you must motivate yourself. If you don't start now, you will wait and wait for that "right moment," but, let me tell you, that right moment will never come. You must make your opportunities and create your circumstances. Just make a decision, stick with it, and just start.

The secret to getting ahead is getting started.

—Mark Twain

JUST FINISH

A proverb from Afghanistan says, "The start of something is a job half done." We all know that starting something is difficult. You need a set of ideas and directions. Starting something productive is important, but seeing it through says a lot about who you are. Importantly, getting in the habit of finishing the task you started will be critical in who you will become and what you will accomplish in life.

We all have heard and known people with great ideas and big dreams, but they have gotten nowhere. Now this doesn't mean they failed to act on what they believed in, but they simply gave up halfway through their project or dream, and that's why they didn't accomplish anything. How many people do we know that have big dreams and great ideas? Plenty.

At this point, we are reluctantly giving yet another example of our dad. About 18 years ago, our dad had an idea to prevent some frauds that the banking industry was experiencing. In 1996, CNN reported there were $56 billion of check frauds in the United States alone. So, my dad presented his idea to the United States Patent and Trademark Office, and he was granted a patent. In those days, people used to write checks for everything, from shopping for groceries to paying bills and to sending a check to a grandchild as a birthday gift. So, he had a chance to make something that would have been useful for everyone at that time. He did the first half but failed the second: marketing and selling it to the banks. In other words, just finish the job. To this day, he tells me, "Just finish the job!"

Don't stop when you are tired. Stop when you are done.

—Unknown

TAKE A WALK

Walking is a great way to get your mind off of things, while at the same time calming yourself. You can walk by yourself or go out with your folks so you can just talk. It feels great and keeps your body healthy and in shape. We walk with our family a lot and talk about our futures, things we can get better at and the problems that we need to fix. That way, we keep ourselves motivated to be better people and have better lives. We are writing this topic right after a nice, long walk. It was both of us with our mom, and we discussed opportunities and things we should talk about in this book. After a long talk about our future and our book, we came up with three topics, and we are now writing them. Take time out of your day to walk and refresh your mind, preferably with your family.

**Pursue some path, however narrow and crooked,
in which you can walk with love and reverence.**

—Henry David Thoreau

OPENING YOUR EYES

Until very recently, I was a person who got distracted easily. I had no focus on my priorities whatsoever. This got to the point where I couldn't do even simple things. Not that I was born this way, but my small bad habits had become a big flaw in my personality. For instance, I would be at school for a free hour, and I would decide to study. On the way to one of the buildings, I would see a friend, stop, and chat him or her up, and the talking would last from five to ten minutes if I was lucky. Then, the next friend would come along, and another ten minutes would go by, and then another, and another, until finally, 30 to 40 minutes would have passed by. I'd look at the time and decide, "Even if I start studying now, I won't have enough time."

This is just how delusional my focus was. When a friend would ask to hang out, I'd say yes, not even knowing whether I was able to. If it turned out I was able to, then great. If not, I'd do everything in my human power to hang out with them anyway because I was too carefree about my priorities, and I didn't want to bother the friend by declining his invitation. I wasn't strong enough to say no to the fun I would have at that moment, but man, the guilt I would feel later was terrible. To make a long story short, I wasted a lot of valuable time.

Did you notice how much I would go through just to see people I don't even talk to anymore, and the fun I set out to have? Unfortunately, since I was so focused on having fun, I didn't see the very things I already had. I was running toward the fun, but sadly I was trampling on things even more important. I was too closed-minded to see. You, reading this book, don't notice what's next to you or around you. Once you look around, then look back at this writing, you can't help but continue to notice what's around. Once I realized how things were around me, I have become much more dedicated to my family and appreciative of my time, rarely wasting it and never again taking my family for granted.

I had been so distracted by short-lived fun that I had forgotten what mattered in my life. My independent personality had driven me away from family, and my lack of focus had taken me away from the correct use of time itself. I had spent a lot of my time with friends, not when I had free time, but when they had it. Yet when I was free, they were never around. When I realized this, I cut nearly everyone out except for a few whom I knew were true friends. But I can't even rely on them. Thankfully, I am not in need of anything.

I have realized a lot of things. I hope you realize and open your eyes to what matters to you. Cherish those things because, once time goes on, you can't get those precious moments back.

One of the greatest titles in the world is parent, and one of the biggest blessings in the world is to have parents to call Mom and Dad.

—Jim DeMint

YOU HAVE THE
CHOICE TO CHOOSE

We make a choice between having a good life or a bad life. Every choice has a positive or negative to it. That part is simple. The things we choose will shape our future outcomes, so we must choose carefully. We all can make ourselves who we want to be, but the struggles of life can interfere with our passions and dreams and hold us back. For us to overcome these obstacles and distractions, we must adopt a way to have a good mindset toward what we want to become, be, or hope to achieve.

Since we're on the subject of distractions, choices should be made carefully when you're in your teens because this is a time when we are going through uncertainties in our lives and facing plenty of peer pressure. Don't make bad decisions that will destroy your future, and don't listen to friends who insist and "dare" you to doing something bad. You will likely never see them again. We have given you plenty of examples of when we have made bad decisions. Almost every one of us makes choices that we wouldn't make now. It's fine to make a mistake now and then—just don't make it a normal behavior.

I was a person that knew right from wrong; unfortunately, some people I was around didn't have that same ability. They made terrible decisions, and I saw these small steps toward failure. I tried to help them, but they never took any of my advice. Since I was in their presence, I would see all their bad decisions and their consequences.

They were not bad people. They were kind, funny and great to talk to. However, they either didn't know right from wrong or chose wrong.

Choices are what make up your life: Choose carefully because the choices you make can either create a great future or set yourself up for failure.

We are our choices.

— Jean-Paul Sartre

DOING YOUR SHARE

From fifth to ninth grade, I slacked so much I even felt guilty all the time. The problem was that it was so built into my character that I couldn't change it. When something was my responsibility, I would never do my share. Yes, I was young, but I still expected better from myself.

As we said in one of our earlier topics, what you deliver you will receive. If you don't do your share in life, you will never reap the benefits. If you do a half-assed job, you will see a half-assed reward. If you put your heart into the thing you do and you do your full share, you will receive the best of benefits from it. That's how life is. There are no shortcuts if you want to achieve a great goal. There is always some form and level of sacrifice you have to make to reach your goal in work.

Start by doing what's necessary; then, do what's possible; and suddenly, you are doing the impossible.

—Francis of Assisi

THE BASIS FOR SUCCESS

Assess your need: This important first part has to do with being brutally honest with yourself. Know the difference between needs and wants.

Do your homework: This task requires focus and consistency. You can be distracted from the work by a friend, a phone call, or other attractive possibilities like the ones the internet pushes before your eyes unexpectedly.

Plan your action: What kind of tools and resources do you need, and who can help you source them out? What kind of expert can you listen to or talk to?

Seek help: When you have done your best but have come to the point at which you either have stopped working toward your goal or have simply been unable to make progress, seek help.

Take action: I can't add anything more to this part other than to remind you of the famous brand that tells you "just do it."

If you want to do something, you will find a way.
If you don't, you'll find an excuse.

—Jim Rohn

AUTHORS' BIO

HEWAD POPAL

As a Running Start Student, Hewad Popal earned his high school degree from Edmonds Heights K–12 and his Associate of Arts Degree in International Relations from Edmonds Community College in 2018.

In 2015, Hewad was selected to participate in the State of Washington's Elite Player Development (EPD) program. In 2016, he competed in the Olympic Development Program (OPD) Championships in Arizona, where he reached the Semi-Finals. In 2018, Hewad played in the National Championship Tournament in Las Vegas, Nevada.

Hewad has traveled to 11 countries and plans to continue exploring the world. He finds invaluable life lessons in nature and among people. He is a true gentleman, natural, skillful and thoughtful.

Imran Popal reached maturity at a young age. He is a go-to person for advice. From a young age, his authentic personality and to-the-point communication skill earned him respect and credibility.

His active lifestyle and authentic sports skills are noticeable to any onlooker. On Halloween in 2016, Imran was playing soccer at the Washington State Soccer Championship when a player missed the ball and collided with him. Imran was hospitalized with a broken Tibia and Fibula.

In 2018, Imran's soccer skills earned him an invitation to "play up" with the 18-year-old team in the National Championship Tournament in Las Vegas, Nevada.

Like Hewad, Imran has traveled to 11 countries and plans to continue exploring the world. Imran finds the fields of international business fascinating.